# TEENS IN VIETNAM

# Teens in Vietnam

## Vietnam

by Gregory Nicolai

Content Adviser: Bruce Lockhart, Ph.D.,
Department of History,
National University of Singapore

Reading Adviser: Katie Van Sluys, Ph.D.,
Department of Teacher Education,
DePaul University

Compass Point Books ✧ Minneapolis, Minnesota

Compass Point Books
3109 West 50th Street, #115
Minneapolis, MN 55410

Editor: Julie Gassman
Designers: The Design Lab and Jaime Martens
Photo Researcher: The Design Lab
Cartographer: XNR Productions, Inc.
Library Consultant: Kathleen Baxter

Art Director: Jaime Martens
Creative Director: Keith Griffin
Editorial Director: Carol Jones
Managing Editor: Catherine Neitge

Library of Congress Cataloging-in-Publication Data
Nicolai, Gregory.
Teens in Vietnam / by Gregory Nicolai.
p. cm.—(Global connections)
Includes bibliographical references and index.
ISBN-13: 978-0-7565-2067-0 (library binding)
ISBN-10: 0-7565-2067-3 (library binding)
ISBN-13: 978-0-7565-2075-5 (Paperback)
ISBN-10: 0-7565-2075-4 (Paperback)
1. Vietnam—Juvenile literature. 2. Teenagers—Vietnam—Juvenile literature.
I. Title. II. Series.
DS556.3.N528 2007
305.23509597—dc22                                    2006005397

A note on pronunciations: Throughout Vietnam, several different accents are used when speaking Vietnamese. The two main ones are Hanoi and Saigon, which differ greatly. The pronunciations in this book are based on the Hanoi accent.

Visit Compass Point Books on the Internet at www.compasspointbooks.com
or e-mail your request to custserv@compasspointbooks.com

# Table of Contents

Hanoi ★

MONGOLIA

NORTH KOREA

SOUTH KOREA

Huang

Yellow
Sea

East
China
Sea

CHINA

Yangtze

BHUTAN

NEPAL

BANGLADESH

PHILIPPINES

VIETNAM

South
China
Sea

Salween

LAOS

THAILAND

Mekong

KAMPUCHEA

Bay
of
Bengal

BRUNEI

MALAYSIA

MALAYSIA

SINGAPORE

INDONESIA

THE EXPERIENCE OF BEING A VIETNAMESE TEENAGER VARIES WIDELY. Some teens work in the rice paddies of the Southeast Asian nation, producing food for the country and helping their families survive. Some teens are already married and starting families of their own. Other teens work in the cities' factories, making clothing or shoes. Some work along the city streets, selling newspapers or fixing bicycles. And many, of course, go to school, studying hard in the hopes of going on to college. Teens from all corners of Vietnam dream of improving their lives and the lives of their families.

Because Vietnam is a young country—more than half of its 84 million citizens are under the age of 25—teenagers and children are right at the center of the activity and change. So whatever a teen does in life, it makes an impact on the future of the country.

Teens in Vietnam are required to attend school until age 15, but by high school, about 50 percent of rural teens have dropped out.

# 1

# Admiration for Education

IT IS ALMOST SEVEN O'CLOCK IN THE MORNING, and a group of teenage girls pedals their bicycles toward school. The white cotton tunics of their ao dais, the uniforms that many Vietnamese high school girls wear, flap behind them in the breeze. Just in time, the group hurries into a classroom crowded with 40 other students, past other girls dressed exactly as they are and boys in blue pants and white shirts.

They find their desks and sit down just as the teacher walks into the room to start the day with a quiz. This is a common beginning to the Vietnamese school day, and the students take turns standing and answering questions about material the class covered the day before.

**ao dai**
ow zigh,
or ow yigh

# Fashion Corner

The ao dai is the customary Vietnamese outfit for teenage girls and women. It consists of long, loose-fitting pants and a tunic that falls to the knees. Traditionally, an all-white ao dai was the usual uniform for female high school and college students. But today, schools are more relaxed, and many girls wear skirts, dresses, and jeans most days. On holidays and special occasions, however, the girls pull out their ao dai.

The ao dai is also worn by women of all ages, with younger women tending toward pastel colors and older women—especially those working in hotels and restaurants—wearing dark blue and purple. Many women wear a Western-style gown for their wedding but change into a traditional red ao dai for the reception. Men occasionally wear a form of the ao dai, usually blue or black, but only during certain ceremonies.

For Vietnamese teens who continue their education into their high school years, school and studies are at the center of their lives. Like young people in other countries, they devote several hours each day to their learning. But some students cannot, or choose not to, devote this time of their lives to education. Even though, legally, they are supposed to stay in school until they are at least 15, many drop out earlier. In fact, one in four Vietnamese students between the ages of 14 and 17 leave school.

## Why Drop Out?

One of the reasons so many students fail to make it to graduation is the difficulty of exams in Vietnam. Starting at the end of elementary school, all students must take a long exam that covers everything that was taught throughout the year. A student who fails to answer 70 percent of the questions correctly can't move on to the next grade. Students who fall behind become frustrated, and many of them simply stop going to school.

The first comprehensive exam comes at the end of fifth grade, when most students are 11 years old. The test covers three whole years, focusing mostly on math, and the student must pass the exam in order to move on to middle school. It places an extreme amount of pressure on the young students. In addition to receiving grades, the students are also ranked in order of their work. Everyone knows where everyone else fits in the ranking, who's first in the class and who's last.

By high school, half of all rural teens have dropped out of school, some because of difficulty with the exams, but many because their families need them to help with farmwork. Many don't see any reason to continue with school—their families can't afford to pay university fees, and farming doesn't require a high school diploma. Also, public school isn't free. Families are required to pay a tuition fee,

**dong**
*dome*

usually about 60,000 Vietnamese dong per year, or the equivalent of about four American dollars. It is a major expense for the majority of Vietnamese families, who make less than 6,428,000 dong (U.S.$400) per year.

The schools are so crowded that students often attend in shifts. Half of the students go to school in the morning and half go in the afternoon. This works because the Vietnamese school day is only four hours long. This schedule may

# Sweeping Students

Vietnamese schools do not usually have custodians. Instead, the students are responsible for keeping the school clean. Each class is divided into groups, and each group is assigned a day to come in early to clean up their classroom by sweeping the floors and taking out the trash.

Students at a school in the middle of the countryside are allowed to leave the building for their lunch break.

sound appealing, but students in Vietnam also go to school six days a week, Monday through Saturday. Saturday serves as a review day, when students go over all of the week's lessons.

In addition to overcrowding, schools face other challenges. In rural Vietnam, many of the schools have barely enough money to stay open. Some of the buildings are run-down, and some even have damage from the American War, known else-where as the Vietnam War. Teachers often have to rely on contributions from community members to get the supplies they need, and most schools have only the bare necessities. For instance, elementary schools don't have playgrounds. But things are improving in the cities and even in some rural schools.

Since the 1990s, foreign countries and organizations have given aid money to help Vietnam improve its schools.

# The American War

The American War, known outside the country as the Vietnam War, began as a conflict over what kind of government the country would have: communist or capitalist. Communist leader Ho Chi Minh started the Viet Minh, or Vietnamese Independence League, in 1941 with the intention of freeing Vietnam from French control. In 1945, he declared himself president of the Democratic Republic of Vietnam. Ho forced the French out of Vietnam in 1954, leaving the country split. The north was controlled by Ho, and the southern Republic of Vietnam was led by Prime Minister Ngo Dinh Diem.

The Soviet Union and the People's Republic of China—both communist nations—supported Ho Chi Minh's communist government, while the United States and its allies— including South Korea, Australia, and New Zealand—supported the Republic of Vietnam. The U.S. government was worried that if Vietnam became a communist nation, then other Southeast Asian countries might as well.

As fighting broke out between the South Vietnamese government and the National Liberation Front (Viet Cong), a pro-communist group in South Vietnam, the United States began sending money, weapons, and military advisers to South Vietnam. In 1965, the United States fully entered the war, sending soldiers and beginning a bombing campaign.

The U.S. military left Vietnam in 1973, after nine years of fighting and the death of more than 58,000 soldiers. According to a peace accord signed that year, both North Vietnam and South Vietnam would continue to exist as separate nations. The North Vietnamese Army broke the accord by invading South Vietnam and taking the capital, Saigon, in 1975. Saigon was then renamed Ho Chi Minh City. Between 2 million and 4 million Vietnamese citizens and soldiers died during the war.

# Teen Scenes

A 15-year-old boy hops on his motor scooter to rush to school in the center of the city. He has a busy day ahead of him—four hours of classes in school, followed by his daily tutoring session. As the son of a middle class family, his future already seems bright. But he cannot risk failing to get into college in a few years. He would like to be an engineer, but he knows it will take hard work and good fortune. Even college graduates face difficulty in finding employment.

In what seems a world away, another 15-year-old also faces a busy day. The young woman will be planting seedlings in her family's rice field in the Red River Delta. For her, formal education has come to an end. It was a major expense for her family, and she is old enough now to help her parents with the farming. In a year or two, she'll likely move out of her parents' home and into a home she will share with her husband. Though the legal age for marriage in Vietnam is 22, the law is rarely enforced in rural areas.

In Hanoi, another teenager prepares to go to work. His job is also exhausting, but it varies greatly from the agricultural work in the country. He faces a day of walking city streets to find customers for his shoe shining business. He will enter shops and restaurants, asking those inside if they would like a polish. Even though he has not yet reached the legal working age of 15, the police will likely leave him in peace to earn his livelihood.

Vietnamese teens' daily lives vary, but a common tie binds many of the country's young people—hard work. Whether they are students, vendors, or farmers, many teens labor for many focused hours.

## High school enrollment and attendance

### Males

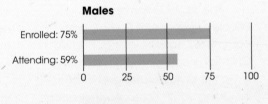

Enrolled: 75%
Attending: 59%

### Females

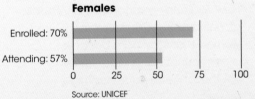

Enrolled: 70%
Attending: 57%

Source: UNICEF

A rural school in northwestern Vietnam serves ethnic minority students.

Hundreds of millions of dollars from the World Bank, the United States, the United Kingdom, and other nations and charitable groups have helped build thousands of classrooms and buy textbooks for rural and poor urban students.

Another program provides children of Vietnam's ethnic minorities with textbooks in their own languages. While Vietnamese is the country's official language, Vietnam's 53 ethnic minorities speak at least that many distinct languages and dialects. These ethnic groups, which together make up almost 13 percent of the population, generally live apart from the Vietnamese majority, in the northern and northwestern hills and mountainous regions and the Central Highlands. Having textbooks in their native language improves these students' abilities to learn.

Foreign agencies are not the only programs coming to the rescue. The Vietnam National Education Trade

Union (NETU), a domestic organization, works to improve schools and education. One recent NETU project was a survey and report, which revealed that "many primary and secondary schools in remote mountainous areas lack the basic amenities, such as classrooms, laboratories, libraries and storage for educational equipment."

The NETU recommended that the government supply more equipment and provide teachers with training on how to use teaching aids. By bringing these educational issues to light, groups like the NETU help to improve school systems in Vietnam.

## Lessons & Homework

Despite challenges, the Vietnamese have a great deal of admiration for education. Traditionally, only members of the royal family were more highly regarded than teachers. Students are expected to take their studies seriously and behave respectfully toward their teachers. The subjects that are stressed most are math, science, and English—subjects that are seen as essential for a good career. In fact, learning to speak English is thought to be so important that some parents start their children in private lessons as 5-year-old kindergartners.

Vietnamese teachers tend to teach rigidly, with little room for personal approaches or variation from lesson plans. Students take turns answering questions aloud or working out math problems at the board. During English

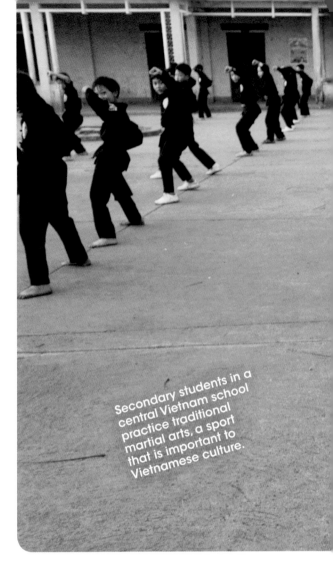

Secondary students in a central Vietnam school practice traditional martial arts, a sport that is important to Vietnamese culture.

lessons, students repeat after the teacher as a group or respond to the teacher's prompts. Answering questions orally and repeating—almost chanting—information are usual activities, partly because neither students nor schools have much money for books and other supplies. Most class activities involve memorizing facts and figures.

High school starts in the 10th grade. Each student can choose from several different programs. Students who want to be scientists can enter a program that focuses on the sciences, while others may choose tracks that stress English, math, or other subjects. In choosing a program of study, Vietnamese 14-year-olds begin to make decisions about their future careers.

## Working Toward a Future

Graduating from high school requires not only high grades and a record of good behavior, but also passing a difficult comprehensive exam that covers material from the previous three years. The exam is actually a series of tests covering chemistry, foreign languages, geography, history, literature, and math. Students who fail the exam either drop out and try to find a job or go to an expensive special school for one year before retaking the exam.

Without a high school diploma, a person can get only low-paying jobs. Because so much of their future depends on passing this test, high school students spend a lot of time studying for—and worrying about—it.

Private tutor sessions or classes at a tutoring center help prepare students for their comprehensive exam. Seventy percent of students between 14 and 21 use private tutoring. Vietnamese teachers do not earn much, making an average of 500,000 dong (U.S.$32) per month. So many of these teachers offer after-school

Vietnamese students have limited opportunities for creative expression; schools don't offer art and music classes. Most students aren't in school-related activities, but many high schools have a few athletic teams. The emphasis is on homework, and parents may get nervous if their teenage children don't seem stressed about schoolwork.

During French colonialism, Lycée Marie Curie was reserved for French high school students. Today, students are Vietnamese.

sessions for a fee as a way to make extra money. Some people claim that the teachers purposely leave out certain lessons when teaching their regular classes just so they will have more customers for night school. Yet many families are willing to pay in the hopes that their children will graduate and, perhaps, go on to college.

Students take the graduation exam in May of their last year of high school, usually at the age of 17.

# A Cheater's Tale

The intense pressure of Vietnam's college entrance exam can get the best of some students, and cheating can be a temptation. In past years, students have created, or even purchased, cheat-sheets to help them with portions of the tests that require memorization.

In July 2006, about 30 students were caught taking a high-tech approach to cheating. They hired a cheating ring, organized by a 39-year-old man from Vinh Phuc province in northern Vietnam. Ring leaders fed them answers to math problems through cell phones and other hearing devices, which were hidden in students' clothing, hair, or even wigs. The students read questions into their phones to a group of college students who then solved the problems within 15 minutes. A third group would then read the answers back to the test-takers.

The Ministry of Education and Training plans to establish a special team to prevent high-tech cheating in the future.

In June or early July, those who want to go to college take another difficult test. This entrance exam is just as long as the graduation exam and even harder. Only 15 percent of the students who take this test are accepted into college. Therefore, formal education for most teens who made it to high school comes to an end at this point.

However, Vietnam's educational system is changing. The government now allows private colleges and universities. There are 123 colleges and universities in Vietnam, and more are added each year. These new colleges, along with improvements in high schools, have allowed the number of Vietnamese students entering college each year to increase from about 100,000 in the early 1990s to around 1 million today.

Those teens who do get into college tend to study just one area because many Vietnamese universities focus on one particular subject, such as a foreign language or engineering. The specialized schools make it difficult for students to get the kind of general training they need for many careers.

Because foreign language study is so important, a Vietnamese student may enter a program in English at one school and a program in law or business at another, earning two degrees at the same time. In addition, some of the newer universities are more general to allow studies in different disciplines.

Two-thirds of all Vietnamese households grow some amount of rice.

# 2

# The Day to Day

MEMBERS OF AN ENTIRE FAMILY—parents, children, grandparents, and others— stand barefoot in the ankle-deep water of a rice paddy. Each holds a small plant with bright green leaves.

Bending over, they carefully plant the seedlings in the mud. They will repeat this process until the whole paddy is filled. Everyone works until, after many hours, it is difficult for them to stand up straight. Families working together are daily sights throughout Vietnam.

Vietnam is a long, narrow country—it is only 30 miles (48 kilometers) wide at its narrowest point. To some, the shape of the country reminds them of a letter S that has been stretched out, but the Vietnamese often describe their country as a pole with a rice basket at each end. These rice baskets are the

# Monsoon Season

Monsoons—constant winds from the ocean that carry heavy rains—determine the weather in Vietnam. In southern Vietnam, the rainy season lasts from April to October, bringing enough water to wash out many of the roads. From May to September, most of the country gets very heavy rainfall. The annual rainfall is more than 40 inches (1,000 mm) all over the country, while the hills get more than twice that amount. When the wind shifts in October, the southern part of Vietnam reaches up to 93 degrees Fahrenheit (34 degrees Celsius) in sunny weather. But in the north, the weather cools to around 70 F (21 C) and stays drizzly. Northern Vietnam has a rainy season and a *really* rainy season.

Mekong and Red River deltas, two of the best places in the world for growing rice. The weather in Vietnam—hot with plenty of rain—is just right for rice. Vietnam, along with neighboring Cambodia, Thailand, and China, is one of the largest rice-producing nations in the world, and most of its people are involved in growing and harvesting this crop.

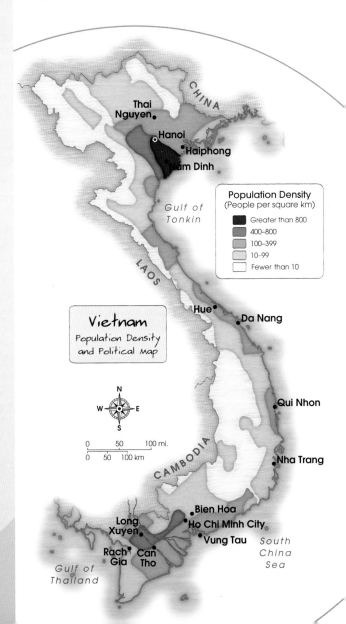

**Vietnam** Population Density and Political Map

**Population Density**
(People per square km)

- Greater than 800
- 400–800
- 100–399
- 10–99
- Fewer than 10

CHINA
Thai Nguyen
Hanoi
Haiphong
Nam Dinh
Gulf of Tonkin
LAOS
Hue
Da Nang
Qui Nhon
Nha Trang
CAMBODIA
Bien Hoa
Ho Chi Minh City
Long Xuyen
Vung Tau
Rach Gia
Can Tho
Gulf of Thailand
South China Sea

N W E S

0  50  100 mi.
0  50  100 km

Fourteen-year-old Nguyen Tien Cuong watches over ducks at his family's farm in northern Vietnam.

## Rural Life

About 75 percent of Vietnamese people live in rural villages. Most of these villages line the channels and canals of Vietnam's two great rivers, and the communities are almost entirely devoted to rice farming. Rural teens help their families with growing and harvesting rice, sometimes quitting school in order to work. There are few job opportunities outside of the cities. In most places, farming is the only way to make a living.

Much of the Vietnamese countryside is green and lush, and the rain and rivers support a wide variety of wildlife, including many varieties of snakes. While some of the snakes are

In northern Vietnam, the Muong minority build their houses on stilts and use bamboo and thatch as materials.

dangerous to people, Vietnamese farmers know that without snakes there would be too many rats, and rats eat rice. Rural Vietnamese understand these things because they depend on the land around them for their everyday needs. Many people live where they can walk to a small market to buy food. But if a family is very poor, or if a family needs food and there is no market down the street to run to, the family may hunt the frogs, rats, and snakes that live on their land.

The traditional Vietnamese house is made of mud, bamboo, or brick and has one main room with two bedrooms on either side and a kitchen built off the back. One bedroom is for the parents and the other for the children. "Privacy" and "personal space" are terms that don't mean much in Vietnam, and most Vietnamese teens share a bedroom with brothers and sisters. It's common for people to enter each other's rooms without knocking.

Many houses, especially in the country, lack electricity and indoor plumbing, often leaving children and teens responsible for gathering firewood and hauling water.

## In the Cities

In addition to the rice fields, the deltas contain Vietnam's biggest cities, Hanoi in the northern Red River Delta, and Ho Chi Minh City, formerly called Saigon, in southern Vietnam's Mekong Delta. These bustling cities hum with the activity of new construction. Noises and fumes from a constant stream of motor scooters and motorbikes fill the air. On days when air pollution from the scooters, motorbikes, and cars is particularly thick, riders wear surgical masks over their mouths and noses to protect themselves against the unhealthy air.

The city streets are also filled with

Motorbikes are the most popular and affordable form of transportation in Ho Chi Minh City.

# Getting Around

Many Vietnamese teens have never driven or ridden in a car. Many families cannot afford one, but cars aren't very practical anyway. Some roads almost disappear during the rainy season, and others are riddled with potholes, making for a bumpy and dangerous ride. In places such as Ho Chi Minh City, people on motor scooters and bicycles sometimes find it impossible to get through the waterlogged and muddy streets. When stuck in a heavy rain, some get a ride for a fee in a *cyclo*, a sort of oversized, backward tricycle with two wheels in front and one in back. Cyclos can often manage the streets during the worst of the rainy season. It gets more stability from its three wheels than a bike or motor scooter gets from two.

Modern apartment buildings and satellite dishes are increasingly common in contemporary Ho Chi Minh City.

**cyclo**
*SICK-low*

bicycle riders going to school and work, from the country into the city and back again. Farmers moving animals to the city markets pack their chickens or young pigs into cages and strap the cages to a bike. It is not uncommon to see motorbikes carrying dead pigs between the slaughterhouse and market.

Women ride bicycles in from the edge of the city, their baskets full of flowers for the markets. Children and teenagers walk along the streets selling newspapers and souvenirs to tourists. Vietnam's cities are hectic and crowded; each day they grow more so as people from the country move to Hanoi, Ho Chi Minh City, Hue, and other urban areas.

A dozen or more family members often crowd together into one apartment. It is common for grandparents, parents, children, aunts, uncles, and cousins to all live together, sometimes in one room. But as families accumulate some savings, they will upgrade their apartments and move to larger homes.

Many urban teenagers are responsible for earning money for the family. If not, they help take care of brothers and sisters or elderly grandparents. The urban families who do not depend on extra income from their teenagers send their children to school, hoping their children will graduate from high school and get better jobs in the city.

The benefits of a higher standard of

In the cities, young people are more likely to dress in Western fashions.

living can be seen in the homes of middle-income and wealthy Vietnamese. Their Western-style houses are more spacious, often two or more stories high, and bedrooms are not shared among as many family members.

## Blending Beliefs

No matter what size the home, its most important feature is the family altar. On this altar, a kind of mantel, the family places photos of deceased relatives, the names of ancestors, and religious items.

In Vietnamese culture, it is believed that the spirits of those who have died can affect the lives of the living. So the Vietnamese pray to their ancestors, asking their help and offering them gifts. This is one of the most important elements of religion in Vietnam.

For Vietnamese, the spirit world is all around. According to tradition, the Vietnamese believe that a person's ancestors are always watching and either approving or disapproving of the way that person lives. Each person has a responsibility to those who came before. In fact, family is so important in Vietnam that it is the basis for religion. With the exception of Christianity, ancestor worship remains important no matter what religion a person follows.

The Vietnamese people also tend to combine elements from different religions. For example, a man might leave rice at a roadside shrine for someone who died in a motorcycle accident and is now thought to be a wandering spirit.

A roadside altar marks the location of a fatal accident in southern Vietnam.

# Cao Dai

The Vietnamese habit of combining religious practices and beliefs is most clearly seen in Cao Dai, a religion that was created in Vietnam in the 1920s. Cao Dai teaches that all religions contain truth and that all people are brothers and sisters. It combines beliefs and rituals from Buddhism, Christianity, Taoism, and other religions and is organized like the Catholic Church.

Cao Dai has a pope, cardinals, bishops, and priests, as well as its own group of saints and holy figures, including Jesus, Joan of Arc, and the French writer Victor Hugo. There are between 3 million and 8 million followers of Cao Dai in Vietnam.

During a Cao Dai mass, the men and women sit and pray in separate sections.

This same person might also pray in a Buddhist pagoda, pray to ancestors for help, and even include an image of Jesus among the holy items almost all Vietnamese keep in their homes. Most Vietnamese feel quite comfortable combining different religions.

Though the constitution of Vietnam officially allows religious freedom, government leaders tend to be wary of it. Nonetheless, about 80 percent of Vietnamese identify themselves as Buddhists. They also practice ancestor worship and animism—a belief that spirits exist everywhere, including in rocks, rivers, and trees. Christians, mostly Catholics, make up less than 10 percent of the population and are less likely to practice ancestor worship or animism.

## What's Cooking?

Whether they live in the country or city, and whether they are Buddhist or Catholic, all Vietnamese have something in common when it comes to their taste in food. Although specific menus may vary from place to place, many of the ingredients are the same.

## Rice for Breakfast

Each morning, as mist rises from the rice paddies and rivers of Vietnam, village women and girls build fires in clay or brick ovens to prepare breakfast. The breakfast dish may be fried rice or rice gruel, similar to oatmeal, made from last night's leftovers.

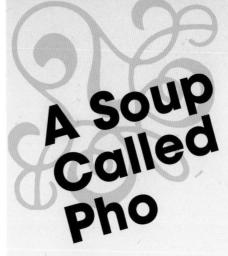

# A Soup Called Pho

One of the most popular dishes in Vietnam, *pho*, can be eaten for breakfast, lunch, or dinner. Boiling hot beef broth is poured into a bowl full of rice noodles and slices of raw beef, cooking the meat. Another common version uses chicken. The soup is flavored with fish sauce, ginger, dried shrimp, and sometimes cinnamon and anise.

The noodles are scooped up with chopsticks, and the broth is eaten with a spoon. However, if the soup is especially good, diners tend to slurp their pho right from the bowl.

Other ingredients such as bean sprouts, lemon juice, herbs, and spicy sauces are served along side the soup, so each person can have the soup just the way he or she likes it. Generally, pho restaurants in the south offer more varieties than those in the north.

**pho**
*fuh*

Or it might be *xoi*, sticky rice mixed with whatever happens to be available—often peanuts or mung beans or, in the south, coconut meat and sugar—all wrapped up in a banana leaf.

Whatever the recipe, the people of Vietnam's villages are sure to have rice before they head off to school or to work in the rice paddies. They also drink tea, which is often grown in the family garden.

**xoi**
*SOH-ee*

**banh mi**
*bine mee*

In Vietnam's cities, the day begins in a different way. From the streets comes the smell of steaming hot soup and freshly baked bread. People rush to offices, factories, and schools, but some stop long enough to buy a bowl of noodles or *banh mi*, a French bread sandwich smeared with a spicy sauce made from ground pork.

A typical serving of pho in Ho Chi Minh City uses thinner noodles and a greater variety of herbs than a serving in the north.

33

Others eat at home, perhaps having rice gruel flavored with meat, fish, or curdled duck's blood. They are just as likely to have French bread with butter, or *pho*, the beef and noodle soup that is one of Vietnam's national dishes.

## Lunchtime

In Vietnam, it is common for the whole family to eat lunch together. Parents come home from work, and children and teenagers come home from school. This practice is changing in the cities because family members keep varied schedules. Many workers and

A variety of foods, including roasted dog meat, can be found at roadside eateries.

students now take a lunch of leftovers with them.

Those with money to spend can visit a roadside stand or an inexpensive restaurant that caters to workers and students. At such a place, friends might share a plate of steamed ravioli or rice with barbecued pork.

If students do make it home for lunch, they can expect rice, a little meat or fish, and soup. In the country, lunch looks a lot like breakfast: rice—probably left over from breakfast—flavored with whatever is available, usually salted eggplant or shrimp paste.

City teens and country teens share at least one habit: napping after lunch. Whether at home or under a tree by a rice paddy, many people, young and old, curl up for 30 minutes to an hour and a half after lunch. In hot-weather countries such as Vietnam, it is common practice for people to sleep during the hottest part of the day. However, this is becoming less common in cities, as more Western-style businesses permit their workers no more than an hour for their break.

## And for Dinner

In a small apartment kitchen, a woman stirs a pot of soup while her teenage daughter cuts pork into bite-sized pieces. A younger girl sets a bamboo mat, called a *chieu*, on the floor of the room where the family eats.

**chieu**
CHEE-ooh

# French Bread in Vietnam?

Every day, mountains of fresh French bread loaves are sold in the cities of Vietnam. The dough is made from scratch, and the bakers take great pride in their bread. Until 150 years ago, though, the Vietnamese didn't eat bread at all. The French brought the art of bread baking with them when they occupied all or part of Vietnam from 1858 until 1954. People in the cities took to the practice, becoming expert bakers. In fact, some visitors to Vietnam say the French bread in Vietnam is better than that in France.

The French influence can be seen in the consumption of coffee and ice cream as well, and in the European-style buildings in cities such as Hanoi and Ho Chi Minh City.

35

Vietnamese delicacies feature ingredients like tofu, fish, pork, and cabbage in soups and main dishes.

Soon the apartment fills with delicious aromas—spicy pork, chicken soup, steamed vegetables, and, of course, rice. Before dinner is served, *ruou nep, bia* (beer), or another alcoholic beverage may be served.

**ruou nep**
*rio nape*

**bia**
*BEE-ah*

Ruou nep is a potent liquor made from rice. There is no minimum drinking age in Vietnam, so teenage boys might have a glass of ruou nep along with their fathers. Men drink more ruou nep than women do, but women do drink liquor and beer.

A raised tray, called a *mam*, is placed on the bamboo mat, and large bowls containing the food are placed on the tray. The family crouches around as the mother and the teenage daughter fill smaller bowls with rice. Every one waits for the father to take what he wants from the other bowls, and

**mam**
*mum*

French-style pastries fill a Vietnamese bakery.

then they do the same, using the large ends of their chopsticks to move food to their bowls and the narrow ends to bring food to their mouths. There are no knives or forks, only chopsticks and spoons. Everyone stays until the meal is finished and then must ask the father for permission to leave.

After dinner, the family eats *do trang mieng*, which means "something to wash the mouth." What each family has for dessert depends on location and income. In the cities, families are likely to eat fruit such as dragonfruit, a sweet member of the cactus family. Those with a little more money to spend can buy French-style pastries or cakes.

**do trang mieng**
*doe chang MEE-uhng*

# Teatime

If two friends order sweet, French-style coffee at a sidewalk café, the waiter will bring a pot of tea on the side. In Vietnam, tea is so important that it is served whether it's asked for or not. Both children and adults drink it throughout the day for the extra energy it gives. In fact, just about the only time tea isn't provided is during meals. This is because soup serves as a kind of beverage, and Vietnamese "drink" their soup, rather than eating it with a spoon.

# Fish Sauce

It takes a long time to make nuoc mam. Barrels are filled with salted anchovies and left to sit. After about three months, workers remove the liquid that has formed in the bottoms of the barrels, and they pour it on top of the solid fish. The barrels sit for another three months before the dark liquid is drawn from the tops of the barrels and sold as fish sauce.

Rural families might have a bit of fruit but most likely will just drink one last cup of green tea as the sun goes down.

## Sea Snacks

*Nuoc mam*, Vietnamese fish sauce, is one of the most important ingredients in the national cuisine. This salty, strong-smelling, light-brown liquid is found in almost every Vietnamese meal. The Vietnamese use it the way other cultures use salt. When mixed with lime juice, chilies, garlic, and sugar, it becomes *nuoc cham*, a popular dipping sauce.

**nuoc mam**
NEUH-uck mum

**nuoc cham**
NEUH-uck chum

With more than 1,000 miles (1,600 km) of coastline, many of Vietnam's favorite ingredients come from the ocean. Because most Vietnamese don't have access to refrigeration, traditional techniques are used to preserve fish. Shrimp and crab are turned into flavoring pastes, and sun-dried squid is a popular snack food.

Other Vietnamese snack foods come from a variety of places. People climb palm trees in search of grubs, which are then rolled in flour, fried, and dipped in nuoc cham. In northern Vietnam, it is common to head down to the village market for some boiled grasshoppers. For many Vietnamese people, especially those without much money, they are a welcome

Sugarcane juice is most often flavored with a squeeze of lemon.

addition to a diet made up almost entirely of rice.

If a thirst needs to be quenched, teens might pick up sugarcane juice. Sugarcane is freshly pressed and sold at roadside stands, often flavored with fruit and served over ice. While Western-style sodas have become popular among teens in Vietnam, sugarcane juice is still a far more common way to beat the heat.

In Vietnam, where 95 percent of vehicles are motorbikes, families are far more likely to travel on motorbikes than in cars.

# 3

# The Love of Family

THE SCENE AT A VIETNAMESE TRAIN STATION IS FAMILIAR to stations around the world: friends and families waiting for their loved ones to arrive. But when the passengers get off the train, there will be no warm embraces. Husbands and wives, though excited to see each other, will share a simple hello, rather than a hug or kiss. Teenage sons will greet their fathers with a handshake. Only small children, young enough to be picked up, will be shown physical affection.

Family members love and care for each other, but in Vietnam there are rules about behavior, especially public behavior. Husbands and wives don't kiss in public or even in front of their children. Generally, parents only hug and kiss very small children. But the lack of physical affection doesn't mean that the parents do not love their children. Vietnamese parents work and sacrifice for their children. Fathers, in particular, are known to give their children gifts whenever they can. "If the children are spoiled, it is because of their father" is a well-known saying in Vietnam.

The family—*gia dinh*—is more important than the individual person. In fact, upon marriage, a woman will usually keep her own family name. Even the way Vietnamese names are written and said reflects the importance of family. In Western usage, surnames are said and written last, but in Vietnamese, the family name is said first, followed by the middle name and then the personal name. For example, someone named Mary Ellen Jones would be called Jones Ellen Mary.

**gia dinh**
*zah ding or yah ding*

For the Vietnamese, the honor and good of the family is everyone's sacred responsibility, and young people are expected to follow the wishes and instructions of their parents. For Vietnamese teens, how they act, what they study, and who they date is heavily influenced by their parents. This Vietnamese idea of family has been strongly affected by Confucianism, a way of life that stresses respect for authority. Within the family, the father is the main authority, although the mother has considerable power as well.

## What's In a Name
Common Vietnamese names and their meanings

### Male Names

| Name | Meaning |
|------|---------|
| Long | Dragon |
| Hung | Heroic |
| Tien | Progress |

### Female Names

| Name | Meaning |
|------|---------|
| Hong | Rose |
| Lan | Orchid |
| Huong | Fragrance |

### Names for Both Genders

| Name | Meaning |
|------|---------|
| Ngoc | Jade |
| Hoa | Peace |
| Giang | River |

# Confucianism

Confucius, or Khong Tu in Vietnamese, was a Chinese teacher who lived about 2,500 years ago. He taught that people should respect and obey those in authority and that those in authority should be just. The Vietnamese first learned of Confucius' teachings from the Chinese who controlled Vietnam for almost 1,000 years. But many of the Confucian elements in Vietnamese culture were borrowed over the centuries after Vietnam became independent. One of Confucius' most well-known sayings might sound familiar to Westerners: "Do not do to others what you would not like them to do to you."

Confucius was born around 551 B.C.

43

Three generations of Vietnamese women in a home near Hanoi

## Sons, Daughters, & Shrinking Families

Traditionally, Vietnamese families were large, with as many as a dozen children. Having a large family meant that the parents would have many descendants to carry on the family line. There would also be plenty of children to care for the parents as they got older. But in the last 30 years or so, Vietnamese families have gotten smaller. Because of over-population in Vietnam, the government strongly encourages couples to have no more than two children.

This policy has been difficult for Vietnamese families to follow because it is seen as very important that each couple have at least one son. One Vietnamese proverb illustrates how many people feel about having children:

"To have one son is to have; to have ten daughters is not to have."

Family focus is often placed on a son. Girls today have better educational opportunities than they used to. However, a daughter may still have to drop out of school and get a job to help support the family, while a son will be expected to stay in school to try to get into college. He will have a better chance at getting a good job and improving the family's status.

A son is also important because he carries on the family line. While a married daughter will leave her own family to join her husband's, the eldest son will share his home with his parents and care for them in their old age. If a couple has no son, however, the oldest daughter is often expected to remain unmarried and stay with her parents.

## Hand in Hand: Friendship & Dating in Vietnam

Parental approval is very important in all areas of Vietnamese life, but especially in dating and marriage. Traditionally, most marriages were arranged by the families of the bride and groom. Sometimes the couple didn't even see each other until the day of the wedding. Today, most people choose their partners, but teens usually won't date someone without their parents' approval.

There is specific dating etiquette that is followed in Vietnam. In rural Vietnam, it is common for boys to walk hand in hand or with their arms over each other's shoulders, but boys and girls do not hold hands with each other. In the cities, it is more common to see teenage couples holding hands and even kissing.

An appropriate first date would be a trip to a café for coffee and conversation. If a couple continues to date, the boy will be expected to meet the girl's family. Usually this means spending the day with them at their home, so they can get to know him and see if he is respectable enough for their family.

This etiquette is changing in the big cities where teens are regularly exposed to ideas from other cultures. But for those teens in the country, the traditional ways are followed. In the rural areas of Vietnam, it is common for youth as young as 17 to get married even though the government encourages people to wait until they are in their 20s. Many teens in the country don't have a "teen experience" like the ones their urban contemporaries have. They move directly from being children to being adults.

Young couples often cuddle on motor bikes along the Song Sai Gon River in Ho Chi Minh City.

A dragon dance is performed in celebration of Hanoi's October anniversary. Local and regional celebrations can be as festive as national holidays.

# 4

# Celebrating Life, Honoring the Dead

**THE VIETNAMESE CALENDAR** is filled with a year of celebrations, beginning with the new year festival of Tet. For many working people, it is the only real holiday of the year, even though the calendar is filled with public holidays and special celebrations.

Festivals in the rural villages of Vietnam may mark the deaths of national heros, folk singing, or the communities' farmers' love of labor. Each play an important role of teaching teens about their country's rich heritage.

Filling in the gaps between holidays and festivals are events such as engagement ceremonies, weddings, and death anniversaries—all reverent times in Vietnamese culture.

## Important Holidays

The dates of some holidays in Vietnam change each year, depending on the lunar calendar. Some vary only a little, but others can move by more than a month.

**Tet**—generally falls between late January and early February

**Founding Day of the Communist Party of Vietnam**—February 3

**International Women's Day**—March 8

**Liberation Day**—April 30

**International Labor Day**—May 1

**Ho Chi Minh's Birthday**—May 19

**Commemoration of the birth, the enlightenment, and the death of Buddha**—May 28

**Day of the Wandering Souls**—falls in August

**National Day of the Socialist Republic of Vietnam**—September 2

**Ho Chi Minh's Death Anniversary**—September 3

**Tet Trung-thu**—falls in September

**Teachers' Day**—falls in November

Tet flags wave in celebration of the new year in Ho Chi Minh City.

A simple Tet celebration at home includes a serving of tea and sweet treats.

## Feast of the First Morning

Family gatherings, gift giving, and feasts of delicious food are all reasons why teens look forward to the Vietnamese New Year, Tet. The date of Tet varies from year to year, depending on the lunar calendar, but it usually falls at the end of January or beginning of February.

The eve of the holiday was once celebrated with lots of fireworks, but after 71 people were killed by fireworks on Tet eve in 1994, the use of fireworks was banned. Some Vietnamese feel that this has taken much of the fun out of Tet celebrations.

On the first day of Tet, families all over the country gather to celebrate a new beginning, welcome the coming of spring, and honor their ancestors. Outside most houses, a *cay neu*, or Tet tree, is erected. Often up to 16½ feet (5 meters) tall, the Tet tree is a bamboo pole that is stripped of its leaves

**cay neu**
*kye NAY-u*

49

and decorated with colored paper, good-luck charms, and wind chimes.

Inside, the homes are thoroughly cleaned and decorated with flowers, peach blossoms, and *hoa mai* petals from the small yel-low blossoms of the apricot tree or the mandarin orange tree. New offerings of fresh fruit are set on the family altars.

**hoa mai**
*hwah my*

Girls often help their mothers pre-pare the traditional Tet food for the day's feast before the rest of the family arrives. Some traditional Tet foods are dried pigskin soup, sticky rice dishes, boiled chicken, stir-fried almonds, papaya salad, bitter melon stuffed with meat, and green bean pudding. Most food is made at home, but some traditional dishes—such as pork head pie, a pork dish called *banh chung*, and cinnamon pork paste—can be bought at mar-kets. *Mut Tet*, a tray of candied fruits, vegetables, and flower petals, is also served, as are betel leaves. Having an overabun-dance of food is such a big part of the new year's tradition that many people ask each other, "Have you eaten plenty of food for Tet this year?"

**banh chung**
*bine choong*

**mut Tet**
*mutt tate*

Families always wonder who will be the first relative to walk through the door. It's important for the first visitor of the new year to be someone who is happy and lucky; many believe that if Tet begins well, then the coming year will be prosperous. The family mem-bers wish each other joy and luck in the coming year, and then the children

# Banh Chung

Banh chung is a cake made from sticky rice, pork, lard, and green bean paste. The ingredients are formed into square cakes, wrapped in bamboo leaves, and boiled for up to 12 hours. Many Vietnamese do not enjoy eating this heavy, fatty dish, but they do enjoy the social aspects of making banh chung. The whole family sits by the fire, telling stories of past New Year celebrations while the banh chung cooks.

and teens receive their *tien mung tuoi*, or lucky money. Each young person gets a red envelope of money from his or her elders, the red symbolizing luck. This money is also known as age-celebrating money, since everyone is thought to turn a year older on the New Year.

**tien mung tuoi**
*TEE-un mung TOO-ee*

Some teens also receive new clothing or other presents.

While age-celebrating money might be the favorite part of Tet for the young, the most important part is the welcoming of the ancestors. During the first three days of the new year, the spirits of ancestors are believed to return to the world of the living. Each family places offerings of food, alcohol,

New Year's prayers are often said at a public temple. The celebrants hold their incense as they pray.

51

and flowers on the family altar. Three sticks of incense are burned while the oldest male in the family kneels and whispers the names of the ancestors. He invites the ancestors' spirits to enjoy the feast. After this ritual, the family sits down, eats, and celebrates.

The second and third days of Tet are spent visiting family and friends, showing off new clothing, and, for young people, finding ways to spend their lucky money. At the end of the third day, the family says goodbye to their ancestors' spirits. Fake money is sometimes burned so the ancestors can pay for their way back to the spirit world. Most people return to school and work after the third day, but Tet doesn't officially end until the seventh day, when the Tet tree is taken down. Even then, the wealthy may continue to celebrate for the rest of the month.

## A Festival for Fall

Children in masks parade through the moonlit streets carrying colorful paper lanterns. The sound of drums and gongs fills the air as teens and adults gather to watch the children and to talk under the full moon.

Tet Trung-thu, or Mid-Autumn Festival, is mainly a holiday for children. Kids go out at night wearing masks and eat sweets called moon cakes. They also form into groups to perform the dragon dance, in which they wear costumes and join together to take the shape of and move like a dragon. The group

Hanoi school children are excited to celebrate Tet Trung-thu.

dances from house to house and shop to shop, receiving treats and money from the adults.

Unlike the fall festivals celebrated in a number of other cultures, Tet Trung-thu has nothing to do with

# Pure Brightness Festival

Another holiday that honors ancestors comes in the spring. Few holidays are as simple or as beautiful as Le Thanh-minh, the Pure Brightness Festival. People visit the graves of their ancestors where they tend the area, burn incense, and offer food and flowers to the spirits of the dead. The holiday is also an opportunity to enjoy nature and welcome spring. Friends might take a walk through the countryside and gather flowers.

ghosts or monsters. In fact, it's one of the few Vietnamese celebrations that has nothing to do with the spirits of the dead.

The focus of this festival is the moon, which is brightest in September.

Ho Chi Minh
(1890–1969)

they chase us, we run away. What fun!"

Since the 1940s, the Mid-Autumn Festival has also been a celebration of good citizenship. Ho Chi Minh, the first president of independent Vietnam, wrote a letter to Vietnam's children during the 1945 festival, starting this patriotic tradition:

*"Today, the Mid-Autumn Festival is yours. It is also a time for you to demonstrate your love for the country and your support for independence ... You must be good, follow your parents' instructions, study hard, and love and respect your teachers and friends. You must love our country. I wish that when you grow up, you will become good citizens who are worthy of our national independence and freedom."*

## 'Tis the Season

The next popular holiday on the Vietnamese calendar is Le Giang Sinh, or "the Festival of the One Who Came Down to Be Born," which honors the Christian holiday of Christmas. However, because less than 10 percent of the population is Christian, few Vietnamese people celebrate the day.

Vietnamese Christians, who are mostly Roman Catholics, go to church on holiday's eve and then gather with their families to eat a traditional dinner of chicken soup. Children leave their shoes by their doors so that Santa Claus will fill them with presents. In the cities, some non-Christian Vietnamese have begun to celebrate

After they have left treats for their younger brothers and sisters, teenagers go out with friends to look at the full moon, talk, and flirt. The moon is thought to control romance, and flirting is rampant during Tet Trung-thu.

Other teens may play innocent tricks. One 17-year-old boy said he and his friends enjoyed playing with water guns during the festival. He added, "All the boys in our neighborhood go out and splash water on the passersby. When

In December, Christmas decorations are common sales items for vendors in Vietnamese cities.

Le Giang Sinh by going out to eat and exchanging gifts. Some even attend services in cathedrals or Protestant churches.

## Engagements & Weddings

Another time of celebration in Vietnamese culture is engagement. The young couple and their families come together to take part in a traditional engagement ceremony at the bride's home. When the young man arrives with his family, they ask permission to enter the house. After the woman's family invites them in, the groom's family present ceremonial gifts such as areca nuts and betel leaf. The gifts are placed on the family's altar, and both families ask the ancestors to approve of the match. Then the families sit down to talk about the potential marriage. Both families must approve of the match and of each other. If not, the marriage is not likely to take place.

At a traditional Vietnamese wedding ceremony, the young bride wears a red ao dai, while the groom wears blue.

This can be difficult if the families differ in status, particularly if the bride's family is of a higher economic class than the groom's.

If the families agree that the couple should marry, the next step is to decide on a day for the wedding. In Vietnam, this is not just a matter of picking a convenient date. As in much of Asia, certain days are thought to be lucky and others unlucky. The families may hire an astrologer to find the perfect date for the wedding. Once a date is set, the couple is officially engaged. The groom's family then gives the bride's family more gifts, which, in rural areas are then handed out to friends and neighbors as a type of wedding invitation.

There is no official of any kind to declare the couple married. Instead, the groom performs a ritual at his family's altar, asking his ancestors for permission to marry. Then he and his family and guests travel to the bride's family's house for similar ceremonies.

Finally, everyone returns to the groom's house, where the couple repeats the ritual once more. The groom's father makes a speech, and the couple is then considered married. However, they must officially register their marriage with the government as well.

Everyone stays at the groom's family's house for a reception with music, food, and drink that lasts long into the night. In cities, many couples

# Betel & Areca

Throughout Southeast Asia, people chew betel leaves and areca nuts for the feeling of energy they give. The effect is similar to that of the caffeine in coffee and cola. In Vietnam, betel and areca are important as ceremonial gifts. However, many people among the higher economic classes avoid actually chewing them because doing so can turn the teeth black. Evidence of chewing betel is found in places other than the chewer's mouth. Visitors to Vietnam will sometimes notice red smears on the sidewalk— betel that chewers have spit onto the pavement.

A new trend in Vietnamese cities is to take wedding portraits before the wedding and present a slide show of the photo shoot at the reception.

hold a wedding banquet in a hotel and wear Western-style wedding clothes, including a white dress for the bride. After a rural wedding, it is fairly common to see the bride and groom ride off on a bicycle, the groom pedaling and the bride holding on to him while she works to keep her red ao dai from catching in the chain.

## Death Ceremonies: Sharing the Sadness

Not all ceremonies are filled with joy. Families also come together in times of death. In the Vietnamese country-side, if a person dies outside of his or her home, the funeral must be held outside—the body is not allowed to re-enter the house. So families will gather outside of their small huts. Though there are some funeral homes in cities, in much of Vietnam, the family is responsible for preparing the body and conducting the funeral. Families clean the body, set it in the coffin, and build a temporary altar for the funeral. It's important that the family members handle the funeral in the proper way; if they don't, they believe the spirit of their loved one will not find peace, but will wander the world of the living.

Soon after a death, friends and neighbors arrive with gifts of incense

In a traditional funeral procession, most mourners cover their heads.

and food. They tell the family that they are there to "share the sadness." The Vietnamese prefer funerals to be attended by many people—it eases the pain and grief for the family and shows great honor to the deceased person.

The next morning, all of the mourners accompany the family to the gravesite, surrounded by the funeral music of a small band or orchestra that joins them. Traditionally, this procession is made on foot, and the coffin is either carried or pushed on a cart. Once at the gravesite, the coffin is placed in the ground, and family members toss dirt onto the coffin before the grave is filled in.

Mourners then light incense sticks and set them on the grave as a sign of respect. After the actual funeral, even more guests arrive at the family's home for a feast in honor of the person who died. People share their memories of the deceased and celebrate that person's life.

## Birthdays & Death Anniversaries

The funeral is not the final time a family will celebrate a loved one. *Gio*, the anniversary of a loved one's death, is acknowledged with a ceremony.

gio
ZO

Relatives fill the home of the leader of the family, usually the eldest male, each bringing a small gift. Everyone gathers around dishes of specially prepared food and waits for the ceremony to begin. The deceased's eldest son, who may be just a teenage boy, performs his most important duty. Standing at the family's altar, he calls on his parent's spirit to

Villagers mourn the death of a well-respected woman in a small community.

**hang ma**
*hahng ma*

detailed models of houses, clothing, money, and even refrigerators and motor scooters, all made from paper or bamboo. Many Vietnamese believe that their ancestors' spirits need these things in the spirit world. On the death anniversary, the hang ma are burned and the items go to the spirit world in the form of smoke.

After the ceremony has ended, the family eats the meal and shares memories of the one who died. The family will continue to gather for this celebration for many years, though it will be most important for the first three. The family may also celebrate a general gio for all deceased relatives around the time of Tet.

While death anniversaries are very important, birthdays are hardly celebrated at all. In fact, the Vietnamese often ignore them completely, because everyone is said to be a year older at Tet. In recent years, some people in the large cities have begun to celebrate birthdays, having been exposed to Western cultures. These birthday parties come complete with wrapped presents and a birthday cake and are celebrated with many friends. Surprise parties are not common among young people; parties are usually thrown by the one having the birthday.

enjoy the feast that has been prepared. The son then lights a stick of incense.

The gifts that everyone has brought are called *hang ma*,

Although the legal age for employment is 15, it is common for younger people to work as street vendors.

# 5

# Growing Rice, Selling Soup

IN HANOI, TEENAGE BOYS WALK UP AND DOWN THE streets trying to chat with passing tourists. Most passersby don't stop, but the boys don't get discouraged. They call out in English, French, and Chinese, hoping to catch a tourist's ear. Occasionally someone will stop for a moment, and a boy will try to sell a postcard, lottery ticket, map, or photocopied book.

He also might offer to show the tourist around, to be a personal guide for a small fee.

This is not a part-time or after-school job. These teens do this all day, every day. Usually the boys have quit school and left their villages for the big city, looking for a way to make a living. Every day children and teenagers leave their families behind and move to a strange place, because there is little opportunity in the rural villages. The only work back home is farming, and many teens hope for the chance to build a better life. Oftentimes their parents encourage them to leave, perhaps hoping they will find work and be able to help the family.

However, because these teens have dropped out of school, they are limited in the kinds of work they can get. Without a diploma, they qualify for only low-paying, often illegal jobs. In addition to selling goods to tourists, these teens will go around the cities, shining the shoes of customers in stores and restaurants. All of it is illegal, because street vendors don't have permits or licenses from the government, and the teens are often under the legal employment age of 15. Sometimes the police crackdown on the illegal activity; other times they are more tolerant.

There are so many young people moving to the larger cities of Hanoi, Ho Chi Minh City, Hue, and Haiphong that a dozen people from the same small village may live and work together. Usually an older person from the village organizes the others, renting a place, likely just one cramped room, where all of them stay. This person also might organize the work, buying and passing out the newspapers to sell and collecting the money. By living together, some of the teens may be able to send a little money home to their families.

As time passes, these teens may find their own work in the city, though

it will probably continue to be illegal. In Vietnam's cities, many people make their living by running temporary businesses along the sidewalks—some sell food, give haircuts, or fix bicycles.

Because the vendors have no shops or storefronts and often move from place to place looking for customers, they have to find clever ways to transport their products and equipment. For example, many women sell soup to office workers and students

A teenage girl transports flowers on her bike. She will sell them on a Hanoi street.

## In the Rice Paddies

Some street vendors may make as little as a dollar a day and must work seven days a week just to survive. So it might be difficult to see why people leave the country villages for the city. But the work they leave behind is rice farming, which is backbreaking, low-paying labor.

who need a quick meal. These women carry everything they need on a pole over their shoulders including the soup pot, bowls, chopsticks, ingredients, and even the means to start a fire to cook the soup.

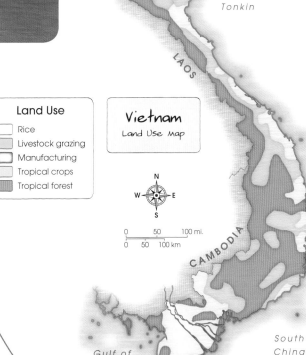

**Land Use**

- Rice
- Livestock grazing
- Manufacturing
- Tropical crops
- Tropical forest

**Vietnam**
Land Use Map

CHINA

Hanoi

Gulf of Tonkin

LAOS

CAMBODIA

Gulf of Thailand

South China Sea

N
W    E
S

0    50    100 mi.
0    50    100 km

## Labor force by occupation

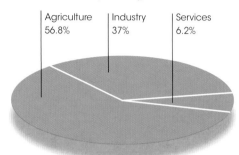

Agriculture 56.8% | Industry 37% | Services 6.2%

Source: United States Central Intelligence Agency. *The World Factbook—Vietnam.*

Many teens quit school to help their families with the rice. While many crops can be raised using modern equipment such as tractors and threshers, rice still needs to be grown and harvested by hand. Part of

Either rain or river water floods the fields before rice seedlings can be planted.

the reason for this is the way in which rice is grown—in paddies, fields that are purposely flooded using canals and ditches.

Basically, a rice paddy is a very wide puddle. Even if Vietnamese farmers had tractors, they wouldn't do much good—the tractors would just sink in the mud. Most Vietnamese farmers use water buffalo to plow their paddies.

# River Deltas

A delta is formed when a river slows as it meets the sea, depositing the silt, clay, and sand it has picked up along the way. Islands form from the deposits, and the river splits into many different channels. The Red River and the Mekong River form broad deltas that are prone to flooding, which fertilizes the soil but can also destroy crops and homes. The Vietnamese control the floodwaters through a complex system of canals and dikes. Paddies are flooded to just the right depth for growing rice and then drained at harvest time.

# Service to the Country

The Vietnamese military drafts young men beginning at the age of 18. Men who come from wealthy or well-connected families can often get out of having to serve. University students are also required to take military training, but this is often seen as a fun break from school. Men and women train together, and social time is mixed with target practice and exercise.

Also, farmers can't plant rice by spreading seeds. Rice needs to grow for at least a month in drier soil. Usually it is grown in special seedling beds. Then each rice plant must be moved to the paddy and transplanted by hand. This is one of the main reasons that rice farming is such hard work and why so many laborers are needed.

## Other Jobs

Though many Vietnamese teens work hard to get into college, Vietnam is one of the poorest nations in the world, and there are not many jobs for college graduates. Vietnam's urban unemployment rate ranges from 6.48 percent to 7.95 percent. Many thousands finish college and are unable to find any kind of professional job. Others can't find work related to their studies and take what they can get. Often they get jobs as translators, making use of their years of English language classes.

Vietnam's cities also offer factory jobs, mainly making clothes and shoes. These factories, some foreign-owned, are often dark and unhealthy. Laws concerning safety or workers' rights aren't always enforced. Employees are expected to work up to 12 hours a day with few breaks. A worker who complains can be fired, and replacement workers are easy to find.

Some factories, of course, are

At Garment Company No. 10 near Hanoi, workers press and pin newly made shirts to prepare them for shipping.

better than others, but none are pleasant places to work.

Other young people without a college education can find work in stores and restaurants. As the number of these types of places increases, the number of jobs for wait staff and salespeople also goes up. Options for working in the service industry are growing.

While some teens hang out at local cafés, others cruise the streets on motorbikes.

# 6

# Cruising, Karaoke, & Carefree Fun

**A SATURDAY NIGHT IN HO CHI MINH CITY BRINGS OUT MOTORBIKES** that carry as many as three teenage passengers. They speed down the main streets, weaving between cars. All night, teens cruise around, looking for friends to meet up with, eager to spend some time away from the watchful eyes of their parents.

For teens from wealthy families, expensive motor scooters provide a way to feel independent, to escape from the pressures of school, the expectations of their families, and their own worries about the future. Though motor scooters are out of financial reach for most Vietnamese teens, many are able to afford the less-expensive motorbikes.

But in the poorer neighborhoods of the large cities, children drop out of school

Chinese chess, a game of strategy, is commonly played in public places.

to sell their wares on the street. By the time they are teenagers, many have full-time jobs. There isn't much room for "leisure time" or "youth culture" in the difficult and busy lives of these teens.

## Entertainment for Everyone

Other forms of entertainment are found at local cafés. As long as customers buy something to drink, they are free to stay for as long as they wish. Karaoke cafés are especially popular in cities. People enjoy singing along to popular songs or watching others take part. Sometimes people go to cafés to listen to music on the radio or played from CDs. Cafés with TVs are also popular gathering places. Customers stop in to see the news or watch a soccer game; others go to talk with friends and perhaps play a game of chess.

Even though access to MTV and pirated foreign CDs has made Western music popular in Vietnam, the music sung in the karaoke cafés and played on the radio is most often Vietnamese pop. The sound of pop music from Europe and the United States has been combined with traditional Vietnamese singing to create the country's most popular music. Well-liked by both teens and adults, songs by pop stars My Linh and Thanh Lam are played constantly on the radio. Vietnamese pop songs are almost entirely love songs and have a soft, sweet sound to them.

Another form of music that has become popular among urban teens is hip-hop. After hearing American rap, teens in cities such as Hanoi and Ho Chi Minh City formed their own groups and started performing. Vietnamese hip-hop uses the rhymes, beats, and even the fashion sense of the American version, but there is one big difference. While the lyrics to American rap songs may contain obscenity and violent language, Vietnamese rap songs tend to be about young love, teenage worries, or humorous situations.

Thai Bao, a Vietnamese high school student, told a news reporter about the trend: "Hip-hop is like a kind of language, which helps us express our personalities."

Another aspect of hip-hop culture

# Government Censorship

The Vietnamese government censors all books, magazines, newspapers, music, movies, and television. Each year, the police seize tons of censored books, CDs, and movies, which are then burned. If the government decides that a novel or song is offensive, the creators of the censored material can be arrested or punished in some way. And while Internet usage is becoming more and more common, some sites are blocked by the government. However, the censors seem to be relaxing somewhat, and Western novels are increasingly available in Vietnamese translations.

73

One of Vietnam's first introductions to hip-hop dancing was from Korean and American exchange students.

that has become popular is dance. Teens form hip-hop dance groups and perform in competitions, often becoming as well known as the musical groups. Some teens save up to buy instructional DVDs and costumes for competitions. The most popular groups compete each year for the right to represent Vietnam in the Battle of the Year Southeast Asia.

This annual contest pits dance groups from Vietnam, Thailand, Cambodia, and other countries in the region against one another.

## Sports

Sports provide other active pastimes, and in the world of Vietnamese sports, soccer is by far the most popular. The national team is followed by most of the population, and the professional teams of the Vietnam Football Federation have fans across the country. People will gather in packed cafés and bars to watch the team on television.

If Vietnam's national team wins over one of the neighboring countries, such as Thailand or Cambodia, people pour out into the streets to celebrate by singing and waving the nation's flag. Young people race their motorbikes up and down the streets, and whole neighborhoods party into the night.

Playing soccer is a favorite activity of many Vietnamese teen boys and girls, but there is a lack of public fields in Vietnam, so pickup games are played in empty lots or on side streets. Generally youth sports are not

The national Vietnamese soccer team (in red) regularly plays against teams from other Asian nations, such as Japan.

organized by adults or the government—there is little money in Vietnam for public sport and fitness activities.

Some of the most popular sports in Vietnam are those that require the least equipment and, therefore, little expense. One of those sports is the Vietnamese martial art, Vo Viet Nam, which uses both unarmed combat, as in karate, and armed combat with weapons, such as the sword, spear, and stick. Vo Viet Nam has developed over hundreds of years, and to practice it shows a teenager's pride in being Vietnamese.

## Movies, TV, & the Internet

For less active pastimes, movies, television, and the Internet fill the bill. If a group of friends heads into a movie theater, they will most likely choose to see either an American blockbuster—

More than 90 percent of urban households in Vietnam own a television set.

action films are particularly popular—or a Chinese martial arts picture. Although Vietnam makes its own movies, they have never been very popular. Until recently, all Vietnamese movies were made by the government. Most of these films had political themes, which failed to interest most moviegoers. While the government still decides what kinds of movies can be shot, the actual movie-making is now done by private companies, which produce more dramas, comedies, and action movies.

As with movies, Vietnamese television is also screened by the government. With the vast majority of urban homes having a television, teens in cities are likely to spend time watching. But TV time is not as important to most rural Vietnamese teens, whose only access to television may be through a neighbor's set. Those who have a TV often invite their friends and neighbors in to watch important sporting events or other popular programs.

Foreign shows are the most popular, and more and more channels are popping up on Vietnamese television. Teens can now tune in to clips from MTV. In the cities, access to foreign channels like the BBC, CNN, and HBO is common. But teens prefer to go out with their friends to the movie theater. Getting away from the family is an important part of hanging out.

Despite the fact that most people do not own a computer, the Internet is very popular in Vietnam's major cities.

Internet cafés are especially popular with urban teens.

# Reader's Den

Just as with television and films, some of the most popular things for young people to read are not Vietnamese. Japanese comic books, or manga, are popular, especially fantasy titles such as *Dragon Ball* and *Teppi*. The Vietnam News Agency reported that of the 600,000 comic books printed in Ho Chi Minh City each week, 80 percent were foreign. The report described many of the comics as "violent stories with rampant killings."

Educators have asked publishers to increase the number of publications that are free of violence and are respectful of Vietnamese culture. Vietnamese comic books are beginning to become more popular, but their less-violent story-lines and artwork appeal mainly to preteen readers.

As for books, the most popular series by far is Harry Potter. Translated into Vietnamese by Ly Lan, a well-known fiction writer, all of J.K. Rowling's books have been widely read by children, teens, and adults.

School children often take field trips to Ho Chi Minh's tomb.

Since 1997, when Internet access first became available in Vietnam, more than 7,000 Internet cafés have sprung up. In cities such as Hue, Hanoi, and Ho Chi Minh City, there are entire city blocks filled with nothing but Internet cafés. Middle- and upper-class teens especially enjoy using the Internet, often spending hours chatting and e-mailing their friends or playing computer games.

## Vacations & Travel

Natural beauty is present in every part of Vietnam, from the seaside villages to the soft green of the countryside to the slow movement of the rivers as they pass through the cities en route to the sea. Most Vietnamese people cannot afford to take vacations alone, but poorer families sometimes travel as a group to save money. Pilgrimages to famous temples and visits to the seashore or large cities are common vacations for these groups. Wealthier families can travel individually or in smaller groups.

Many people travel to Hanoi to visit the mausoleum of Ho Chi Minh. When the leader died in 1969, his body was embalmed. After the American War ended, the communist government built a large stone tomb and placed Ho Chi Minh's body on display. Visitors to the tomb must dress modestly: Women are to cover their shoulders, and all hats must be removed. Somber guards escort visitors through the tomb.

Another popular destination, particularly for citizens of Ho Chi Minh City, is Vung Tau, a resort town on the South China Sea. Vung Tau has a number of attractions, including beautiful beaches, a French mansion, and a 90-foot-tall (144 km) statue of Jesus. The statue, which was built by the local Catholic community, has a spiral staircase that tourists use to climb up to the statue's head for a view of the ocean and surrounding countryside.

A popular place to visit in Central Vietnam is the ancient city of Hue, Vietnam's last royal capital. It is known for the beautiful Perfume River and the man-made beauty of the Citadel, where the last emperors of Vietnam held court. Farther north, people visit Halong Bay where almost 2,000 rocky islands rise dramatically from the water. Many of the larger islands contain caves, which visitors enjoy exploring.

Legend says the islands of Halong Bay were created when a dragon ran through the mountains, cutting the land with his tail.

# Ho Chi Minh Highway

Because the roads in Vietnam are so unreliable, it can take a long time to get from place to place. It is a problem that affects more than just vacations. In some remote villages, there are no permanent roads. The rivers and canals provide the only means of transportation, and towns are cut off from each other. Some people may live their whole lives and never see more of the world than the few miles surrounding their house and village.

But Vietnam is changing, and the government is building new, modern highways to improve the country. The biggest of these projects is the construction of the Ho Chi Minh Highway. During the American War, the North Vietnamese Army moved its soldiers and supplies along a complex of trails running through parts of Vietnam, Laos, and Cambodia known as the Ho Chi Minh Trail. Even though it was bombed many times by U.S. planes, the trail was always rebuilt and was used all through the war. The new highway is being built along the main Vietnamese section of the trail.

**Vietnam Topographical Map**

CHINA
Red River
Hanoi
Red River Delta
Gulf of Tonkin

— Major highway

Truong Son Range
LAOS
Perfume River
Trans-Asia Highway
Ho Chi Minh Highway

N
W E
S

0    50    100 mi.
0    50    100 km

CAMBODIA
Central Highlands

Mekong R.
Mekong Delta
South China Sea

Gulf of Thailand

# Looking Ahead

**LIFE IS CHANGING FOR ONE OF THE POOREST COUNTRIES IN THE WORLD.** Hope for a different future drives young people to move forward in their efforts to create a better Vietnam, and many Vietnamese believe that life is improving. The view that the future is bright is common among the young people, who are the first generation in many years to grow up without memories of war. The teens of today know about the American War only through history books and the stories their parents and grandparents tell. The government of Vietnam is still controlled by the Communist Party, but today's teens are growing up in a time when the government has started allowing people more freedom to choose the life they want to live. Vietnam still has many problems. But many of its young people believe that those problems will be solved and that they might help to solve them.

**Official name:** Socialist Republic of Vietnam

**Capital:** Hanoi

## People

**Population:** 84,402,966

**Population by age group:**
0–14 years: 27%
15–64 years: 67%
65 years and over: 5.8%

**Life expectancy at birth:** 70.85 years

**Official language:** Vietnamese

**Other common languages:** English, French, Chinese, Khmer

**Religion:**
Buddhist: 9.3%
Roman Catholic: 6.7%
Hoa Hao: 1.5%
Cao Dai: 1.1%
Protestant: 0.5%
Muslim: 0.1%
None: 80.8%
Many people follow some Buddhist practices but do not identify themselves as Buddhists

**Legal ages**
Alcohol consumption: no minimum age
Employment: 15
Marriage: 22 (seldom enforced)
Military service: 18

## Government

**Type of government:** Communist

**Chief of state:** President, elected by the National Assembly

**Head of government:** Prime minister, appointed by the president

**Lawmaking body:** Quoc-Hoi (National Assembly), elected by popular vote

**Administrative divisions:** 59 provinces and five municipalities

**Independence:** September 2, 1945 (from France)

**National symbol:** Bronze drum

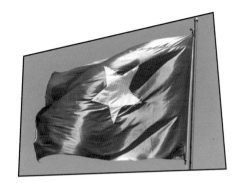

## Geography

**Total Area:** 131,824 square miles (329,560 square kilometers)

**Climate:** Tropical/monsoonal; very hot in the south and cooler in the north; the rainy season extends for approximately six months depending on the region, usually from May through September

**Highest point:** Fan Si Pan 10,375 feet (3,144 m)

**Lowest point:** South China Sea coastline, sea level

**Major rivers:** Mekong, Red, Perfume

**Major landforms:** Central Highlands, Mekong River Delta, Red River Delta, Truong Son mountain range

## Economy

**Currency:** Vietnamese Dong

**Population below poverty line:** 19.5%

**Major natural resources:** Phosphates, coal, manganese, bauxite, chromate, offshore oil and gas deposits, forests

**Major agricultural products:** Rice, coffee, rubber, cotton, tea, pepper, soybeans, cashews, sugar cane, peanuts, bananas

**Major exports:** Crude oil, marine products, rice, coffee, rubber, tea, garments, shoes

**Major imports:** Machinery and equipment, petroleum products, fertilizer, steel products, raw cotton, grain, cement, motorcycles

# Historical Timeline

France seizes control of
Vietnam and combines
it with the present-day
nations of Thailand, Laos,
and Cambodia to form
the colony of French
Indochina

 Inca civilization
flourishes in
South America

The kingdom of
Nam-Viet is founded;
its territory consists of
modern-day northern
Vietnam and parts of
southern China

 World War II

 British colonies
are established
in North America

| 331 B.C. | 207 B.C | 111 B.C. | A.D. 939 | C. 1000 | 1600s | 1884 | 1914–1918 | 1939–1945 |
|---|---|---|---|---|---|---|---|---|

Vietnam fights for and
wins independence
from China

French and Portuguese
merchants and
missionaries set up
trading posts and
churches in Vietnam;
thousands of
Vietnamese convert
to Christianity

 Alexander the Great
conquers Egypt

China conquers Nam-Viet and
adds it to the Chinese empire;
China rules Vietnam for almost
1,000 years

 World War I

🌐 Historical World Event

Saigon, the South
Vietnamese capital, falls
to the North Vietnamese
army, and Vietnam
is reunited as a
communist country;
Saigon is renamed
Ho Chi Minh City

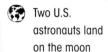 Two U.S.
astronauts land
on the moon

 The Korean War

The United States signs
a peace accord with
North Vietnam, and
American troops
leave the country

The Vietnamese defeat
the French; meant as a
temporary solution, the
country is divided into the
communist North and the
democratic South

The United Nations
is established

| 1941 | 1945 | 1946 | 1950–1953 | 1954 | 1959 | 1965 | 1969 | 1973 | 1975 |
|---|---|---|---|---|---|---|---|---|---|

The United States sends troops to
Vietnam in an attempt to stop
the spread of communism;
thousands of American soldiers
and millions of Vietnamese
soldiers and civilians die in
the war, sparking a strong
antiwar movement in the
United States

France begins an eight-year
war with Vietnamese forces
in an attempt to regain total
control of Vietnam

Ho Chi Minh, a communist,
organizes groups to fight for
Vietnamese independence

Conflict breaks out
between North and South
Vietnam, marking the
beginning of the American
War (Vietnam War)

# Historical Timeline

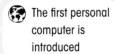 The first personal computer is introduced

Vietnam completes its section of the Trans-Asia Highway

The government relaxes its control over business and allows individuals to start their own companies

 Huge tsunami strikes nations bordering the Indian Ocean

| 1978 | 1981 | 1986 | 1991 | 1995 | 2004 | 2006 |

After a series of violent attacks along its border with Cambodia, Vietnam invades its neighbor; many nations cut all business ties with the country and Vietnam's economy is severely damaged

Vietnam and the United States normalize diplomatic relations

 Soviet Union collapses

# Glossary

| | |
|---|---|
| **amenities** | items that add pleasantness or comfort |
| **capitalist** | a supporter of an economic system in which property is owned by individuals |
| **censors** | examines in order to suppress or remove any information considered objectionable |
| **communist** | a supporter of an economic system in which property is owned by the government or community and profits are shared |
| **comprehensive** | broad in scope; including everything |
| **contemporaries** | people who are about the same age |
| **dialect** | a form of a language that is spoken in a particular area or by a particular group of people |
| **etiquette** | rules that outline proper behavior |
| **grubs** | wormlike larva of certain beetles and other insects |
| **lunar calendar** | a calendar that is based on the cycles of the moon |
| **mausoleum** | a stately and magnificent tomb |
| **prosperous** | having achieved success |
| **rampant** | unrestrained |
| **silt** | mud, clay, or small rocks deposited by a river |
| **tolerance** | the acceptance of people's beliefs or actions that differ from one's own beliefs or actions |

# Additional Resources

## IN THE LIBRARY

Caputo, Philip. *10,000 Days of Thunder: A History of the Vietnam War*. New York: Atheneum Books for Young Readers, 2005.

Parker, Edward. *Vietnam*. New York: Facts on File, 2005.

Phillips, Douglas A. *Vietnam*. Philadelphia: Chelsea House Publishers, 2005.

Seah, Audrey. *Vietnam*. New York: Benchmark Books, 2004.

Sheen, Barbara. *Foods of Vietnam*. Farmington Hills, Mich.: Kid Haven Press, 2006.

Taus-Bolstad, Stacy. *Vietnam in Pictures*. Minneapolis: Lerner Publications, 2003.

Willis, Terri. *Vietnam*. New York: Children's Press, 2002.

## ON THE WEB

For more information on this topic, use FactHound.

1. Go to *www.facthound.com*
2. Type in this book ID: 0756520673
3. Click on the *Fetch It* button.

**Look for more Global Connections books.**

| | |
|---|---|
| *Teens in Australia* | *Teens in Kenya* |
| *Teens in Brazil* | *Teens in Mexico* |
| *Teens in China* | *Teens in Russia* |
| *Teens in France* | *Teens in Saudi Arabia* |
| *Teens in India* | *Teens in Spain* |
| *Teens in Israel* | *Teens in Venezuela* |
| *Teens in Japan* | |

# Source Notes

Page 18, column 1, line 5: "Schools Lack Necessary Teaching Aids: NETU." *Vietnam News.* 29 May 2006. 10 June 2006. http://vietnamnews.vnagency.com.vn/showarticle. php?num=01EDU290506

Page 42, column 1, line 8: Mark W. McLeod and Nguyen Thi Dieu. *The Culture and Customs of Vietnam.* Westport, Conn.: Greenwood Press, 2001, p. 140.

Page 44, column 2, line 1: Kanwaljit Sain. "Challenges for Men and Women in a Changing Society." Asia-Europe Foundation, 2002. 3 March 2006. www.asef.org/documents/S01_Soin.pdf, p. 10.

Page 50, column 1, line 36: "Customs That Never Die." *Vietnam News Agency.* 29 January 2006. 10 June 2006. http://vietnamnews.vnagency.com.vn/showarticle. php?num=01KAL290106

Page 54, column 1, line 10: Nguyen Van Huy and Laurel Kendall, eds. *Vietnam: Journeys of Body, Mind, and Spirit.* Berkeley: University of California Press, 2003, p. 106.

Page 54, column 2, line 9: Ibid., pp. 95–96.

Page 73, column 2, line 13: Trung Hieu. "Is Hip-hop Mere Fashion or a Dangerous Trend?" *Vietnam News.* 7 March 2005. 10 June 2006. http:// vietnamnews.vnagency.com.vn/showarticle.php?num=01TAL030705

Page 78, line 12: "City Parents Worry about Violent Entertainment." *Vietnam News.* 18 June 2004. 10 June 2006. http://vietnamnews.vnanet. vn/2004-06/17/Stories/13.htm

Pages 84–85, At a Glance: United States. Central Intelligence Agency. *The World Factbook—Vietnam.* 13 June 2006. 21 June 2006. www. cia.gov/cia/publications/factbook/geos/vm.html

# Select Bibliography

*Assignment: Southeast Asia*. Dir. Ed Fitzgerald. Christian Science Publishing Society, 1992.

"At a Glance: Viet Nam." UNICEF. 21 Aug. 2006. www.unicef.org/infobycountry/vietnam_statistics.html

"Cao Daism." Religious Movements at the University of Virginia. 15 Jan. 2006, http://religiousmovements.lib.virginia.edu/nrms/caodaism.html

"The Citadel." Vietnam Entertainment Network, 2003. 18 Jan. 2006. www.vietscape.com/travel/hue/citadel.html

"City Parents Worry about Violent Entertainment." *Vietnam News*. 18 June 2004. 10 June 2006, http://vietnamnews.vnanet.vn/2004-06/17/Stories/13.htm

"Customs That Never Die." *Vietnam News Agency* 29 January 2006. 10 June 2006. http://vietnamnews.vnagency.com.vn/showarticle.php?num=01KAL290106

Denney, Stephen. "Banned Books and Other Forms of Censorship in Vietnam During 2002." 13 June 2006. www.ocf.berkeley.edu/~sdenney/vnban.txt

Huynh, Phung Thi. Personal interview. 20 Jan. 2006.

"It's Merry Christmas in Vietnam." *Vietnam News Agency*. 25 Dec. 2005. 28 Dec. 2005. http://vietnamembassy.us/news/story.php?d=20051227175829

"Learn about Vietnam: Vietnamese Culture." Embassy of the Socialist Republic of Vietnam in the United States of America. 28 Dec. 2005. www.vietnamembassy-usa.org/learn_about_vietnam/culture/

McLeod, Mark W., and Nguyen Thi Dieu. *The Culture and Customs of Vietnam*. Westport, Conn.: Greenwood Press, 2001.

*My Hanoi*. Dir. Thuy Linh. Bullfrog Films, 2001.

Nguyen Van Huy and Laurel Kendall, eds. *Vietnam: Journeys of Body, Mind, and Spirit*. Berkeley: University of California Press, 2003.

"Schools Lack Necessary Teaching Aids: NETU." *Vietnam News*. 29 May 2006. 10 June 2006. http://vietnamnews. vnagency.com.vn/showarticle. php?num=01EDU290506

"Senior Secondary Final Exams Begin under Strict Supervision." *Vietnam News*. 6 Jan. 2006. 10 June 2006. http://vietnamnews.vnagency.com.vn/ showarticle.php?num=01EDU010606

Sain, Kanwaljit. "Challenges for Men and Women in a Changing Society." Asia-Europe Foundation, 2002. 3 March 2006. www.asef.org/documents/S01_ Soin.pdf

Slater, Judith I., ed. *Teen Life in Asia*. Westwood, Conn.: Greenwood Press, 2004.

Trung Hieu. "Is Hip-hop Mere Fashion or a Dangerous Trend?" *Vietnam News*. 7 March 2005. 10 June 2006. http://vietnamnews.vnagency.com.vn/ showarticle.php?num=01TAL030705

United States. Central Intelligence Agency. *The World Factbook—Vietnam*. 13 June 2006. 21 June 2006. www. cia.gov/cia/publications/factbook/geos/ vm.html

"Vietnam." World Education Services-Canada. 6 May 2004. 9 Jan. 2006. www.wes.org/ca/wedb/vietnam/ vmedov.htm

*Vietnam: The Next Generation*. Dir. Sandy Northrop. Wind and Stars Production Group, 2005.

# Index

**About the Author**
**Gregory Nicolai**

Gregory Nicolai is a nonfiction writer and poet from Flint, Michigan. He lives in Mankato, Minnesota, where he teaches composition and creative writing at Minnesota State University.

**About the Content Adviser**
**Bruce Lockhart, Ph.D.**

We were fortunate to have Dr. Lockhart serve as our content adviser for Teens in Vietnam. He has spent years researching Southeast Asia, and has a particular interest in Vietnam—previously living there, still visiting often. In fact, during his review of the text he wrote, "I was ... sitting in downtown Hanoi in 2006 and reading through the text!" A professor in the Department of History at the National University of Singapore, he hopes to eventually work on a textbook history of Vietnam, which would allow readers to "learn as much as they can about my favorite country without falling asleep."